**TheOpen
University**

Dyslexia Toolkit

A resource for students and their tutors

Vicki Goodwin and
Bonita Thomson

This publication has been written by Vicki Goodwin and Bonita Thomson and produced by the Student Services Communications Team on behalf of the Open University Centre for Educational Guidance and Student Support.
It updates and builds on the earlier publication *Adult Students and Dyslexia* (1995).

The Open University
Walton Hall
Milton Keynes
MK7 6AA

First published 2001

Edited, designed and typeset by The Open University.

Printed in the United Kingdom by Thanet Press Limited, Margate, Kent.

ISBN 0 7492 39476

Contents

Preface

This book is for anyone who has an interest in dyslexia. It is likely to be particularly useful to students and tutors. It was written by members of the Open University and reflects the experience of OU students, but we hope that other students and tutors will find its suggestions helpful too. Activities and ideas to try out are spread through the book, except Activities 3 and 4, which take a lot of space and so for convenience have been placed in an appendix at the end.

Acknowledgements

The two definitions of dyslexia in section 1.1 come, respectively, from R. Reason *et al. Dyslexia, Literacy and Psychological Assessment* (draft report of a British Psychological Society working party, 1999) and Miles 1993. The distinction between 'composition' and 'transcription' adopted in section 3.3.5 was made by Frank Smith in *Writing and the Writer* (1982, Heinemann).

We wish to thank members of the Open University's Dyslexia Working Group and Antonia Weston BSc (Open) for critical reading of the draft and for their constructive comments. Illustrations by Rupert Rand.

How to use this book

If you've come to this book because you are a student, you've probably got a great deal of other reading to do as well. Don't feel you need to read straight through the book from start to finish. You can get plenty out of it by dipping into whichever sections are appropriate to your immediate concerns. The contents list should help you to do this.

If you are a tutor, we suggest that you start by reading sections 1 and 6, then look at the other sections as the need arises, though we do recommend skimming through them now to get a general idea of the kinds of strategy students find useful.

Both students and tutors will find it helpful to work on some activities together and discuss their outcomes.

SECTION 1
WHAT IS DYSLEXIA?

1.1 Defining dyslexia

We have chosen to say 'dyslexia' rather than 'specific learning difficulties' for several reasons. It is shorter, more familiar to the general population and, we think, more positive. Dyslexia brings difficulties with it, some quite severe, but it also brings strengths and talents. Whatever you call it, it lies at the root of a wide range of learning strengths and difficulties, and no two people experience it in exactly the same way.

The definition of dyslexia has changed over the years and no single definition is universally accepted. In early childhood dyslexia may be suspected if 'fluent and accurate word identification and/or spelling develops very incompletely or with great difficulty'. You may be able to identify with this definition from your own experience as a child. For adults we like the definition that recognizes dyslexia as 'including a set of distinctive talents which can be explained by neurological differences'.

Recent investigations into how the brain works show that the dyslexic brain processes some information in a different way than other brains. The difference gives clear advantages in some cognitive and creative areas, though it also creates difficulties. The dyslexic brain can tackle some tasks better because the right hemisphere, the side of the brain that is responsible for creativity, appears to be more developed in many dyslexics than the left side, which is mainly responsible for acquiring language. Research in this exciting area is still going on. It is already apparent that dyslexia has a neurological cause, affecting language-processing, short-term memory and retrieval of information. The difficulties arise because dyslexic people have to operate in a world in which communication has developed in ways that suit the non-dyslexic majority. Now that we know this, it is more acceptable to 'identify' rather than to 'diagnose' dyslexia.

1.2 Effects of dyslexia

No one person will experience all the difficulties that can be associated with dyslexia. Almost everyone will experience some of them, but people with dyslexia will encounter many. In adults the difficulties are to do with:

Reading, which is likely to be slow

Concentration, which tends to fluctuate

Spelling and grammar, which can be unorthodox

Physical coordination and handwriting

Remembering information

Organizing and planning

Working within time limits

Thinking and working in sequences

Visual difficulties such as blurring and distortion of print

About 1 person in 10 of the general population has trouble with spelling and memory, but some people, about 1 in 25, experience difficulties that have a moderate to serious effect on their whole lives. These people are likely not to achieve their full potential unless they develop compensating strategies and have appropriate support and encouragement.

1.3 Recognizing dyslexia

Characteristics of handwriting that may suggest dyslexia:

- Use of UPPER-CASE exclusively or randomly.
- Letters back to front.
- Irregular size or awkward shape of writing, poor spacing.

Now that so many people use word-processors, examples of handwriting may be hard to come by. But written work can still show dyslexic characteristics even when word-processed or typed:

- Random or non-existent punctuation.
- Missing letters or words.
- Spelling errors: the same word spelt in different ways, letters in the wrong order, phonic approximations, omission of syllables, errors in suffixes.
- Use of similar but wrong words – malapropisms.
- Non-standard sentence structure, an impression of inexperience in writing.
- Misinterpretation of questions.

Some examples of dyslexic writing

Example A

Wan I tried to improf my writing I fownd that my splling
was like the sownd of the words butt I coud not remember
the shaps of the letters

Example B

I have wanted to study for a long time, but no-one would give me help
with my dyslexia by providing photocopied notes. Not being able to get
qualifications has meant that I have not been able to progress in my
career. Now I am studying for the course work from tapes and the
tutors are giving me photocopied notes of tutorials.

Example C

I have been with the open university for three years now having past my my first foundation course T102 last year. I am currently in the middle of D103 that is Social Science which I am thorouly enjoying. The tapes of the course that the OU do send for the course, Namely for reading are a tremendous help. My main Difficulty is Recal AND Sequencing, both of which I find very Difficult. Not been able to transfor my clear Thoughts on to paper easily is a great frustration.

I have been with the Open University for three years now having passed my first foundation course T102 last year. I am currently in the middle of D103 that is the Social Science course – which I am thoroughly enjoying. The tapes of the course that the Open University send me for the course, namely for reading, are a tremendous help. My main difficulty is recall, and sequencing, both of which I find very difficult. Not being able to transfer my clear thoughts on to paper easily is a great frustration.

What is Dyslexia?

Other indications of dyslexia can include:

- Difficulties in remembering and following instructions (directions, for example).
- Variable sense of timing and time management.
- Problems with organizing materials.
- Other short-term memory problems such as dealing with sequences.
- Good days and bad days.

2.1 What are the challenges?

Many dyslexic adult students can read reasonably well and have developed their own compensating strategies, although they struggled with reading and writing as children. Bad experiences in education can lower your confidence and self-esteem. Perhaps you worry that your erratic spelling will make a bad impression, or will misrepresent your meaning. You may avoid certain words altogether, restricting what you would otherwise be able to say. We know that regular encouragement and support from tutors and others is invaluable, enabling students to blossom academically and to achieve their goals. Recognizing and building on your coping strategies is a good way to help you to progress.

Many of the challenges of study are shared by other students, who perhaps haven't studied for a long time or who never developed good reading and note-taking skills at school. But studying presents different or more intensive challenges if you are dyslexic. Reading and re-reading text to decode it – to recognize combinations of letters – reduces the energy that goes into grasping the meaning. Materials that introduce new ideas and new vocabulary may take you twice as much time and effort as another reader. Writing and making notes may be the most difficult thing to do. All these tasks may double the typical workload of a more experienced and non-dyslexic student.

Activity 1
Your concerns

Here are comments that other students have made. You might like just to tick those you share. Later on you could try this again, perhaps after your first few months of study, and see whether anything has changed.

Some of these concerns are expressed by all students, not only the dyslexic ones. People who haven't studied for a long time, or who feel that they never got much out of their schooling, are particularly likely to share them.

Writing:

'I never seem to be able to put down what I am thinking'

'I know what I want to say but I can't find the right words'

Reading:

'I simply can't remember what a word looks like'

Taking notes:

'I can't read my own notes most of the time'

'I start taking notes, but trying to spell words correctly is so tiring, I never get very far'

Spelling:

'Sometimes I spell a word correctly and in the very next sentence, misspell it. But both spellings look the same to me'

'I feel so embarrassed about my spelling – and worry that tutors will think I am lazy as they did at school'

Proofreading:

'Proofreading is a nightmare – I spend hours looking words up, again and again. I still miss things and I can't always work out what I was trying to write'

Organization:

'Finding different forms, assignment booklets, timetables for tutorials etc is chaotic. Information seems to be stored in several different places and if I put it down in the wrong place that's it'

Maths:

'I tend to leave out a digit and then of course it all goes wrong'

Other:

'Some days it seems much harder than others '

'Sometimes I feel really angry that it is so hard to write it down, when I know I understand it just as well as the others'

2.2 Reading

Undertaking almost any kind of study inevitably means that there's going to be a lot of reading to do. Studying with a distance-learning institution such as the Open University means more reading, on paper or on computer screen, than might be necessary at more traditional institutions, where there are greater opportunities to learn from tutors and lecturers in person. The reading material is carefully selected, so you'll spend less time searching for the relevant articles and information. The work is also more structured, with clear instructions for study tasks and suggestions for allotting time to them, and as a dyslexic student you'll probably find that helpful too. But reading is still a fundamental part of study.

If you have trouble with reading, it may be because of visual discomfort and distortion of print on the page. A white page may glare, causing eye-strain or headaches. Words may appear to move, to jumble or to blur. Shadows may seem to fall across the page. All this interferes with reading, and is likely to reduce your attention and concentration.

Some examples of what print can look like:

Robinson and Conway (1988, unpublished) ... significant improvement in subjects using ... school basic academic subjects reading comprehension, reading accuracy, but not in rate of reading. Adler and Atwood (1987) evaluated the results of ten lessons on 23 remedial high school students and a matched control group. Significant improvement for the experimental group was noted for time needed to locate words on a printed page, timed reading scores, length of time for sustained reading, and span of focus, as well as other perceptual tasks. Additionally, seven of the 23 experimental found employment, but none of the control group was employed by the end of the semester.

In contrast, Winters (1987) was unable to find differences in his study. Winters gave 15 elementary school children four minutes to locate and circle 68 examples of the letter "b" on three pages, each page of which contained 600 random letters in 20 lines of

Distortions can be caused by a deficit in the binocular vision system, so you need to get that checked first. Distortion experienced by people whose sight is otherwise perfect is sometimes described as the 'Meares-Irlen syndrome'. You may have heard it referred to as 'scotopic sensitivity'. Its effects can be reduced or eliminated by wearing tinted glasses. The glasses sometimes improve fluency in reading, and sometimes simply help people to read for longer without eye-strain.

The best colour for the glasses varies from person to person. Some high-street opticians, as well as specialist clinics, use an 'intuitive colorimeter' to find out what colour lenses are most effective for you. They can be expensive, but the possibility is worth exploring.

A less expensive solution is overlays – thin clear acetate sheets – in various colours. Some people find these very helpful. You can get special sheets from Irlen-trained screeners and from the Institute of Optometrists, but cheap coloured sheets are sold in ordinary stationery shops. Try out different colours: slide the sheet over the print you want to read, and see whether it makes an improvement. The difference can sometimes be dramatic. If so, it might be worth considering the coloured lenses.

Some strategies to help with aspects of reading other than the purely visual are suggested in section 3.3.1.

2.3 Time for study

Finding and organizing time for study is a challenge for every student, but an even bigger one if you are dyslexic. You'll have dates to meet for essays and other assignments. You might be wise to allow twice the recommended time for each new study task, during your first course at least. If you can do that, it will relieve the pressure and give you scope for developing new strategies.

If you're studying part-time you may have to fit your study in between work and family responsibilities. Adult students have other demands in their lives as well as their study, and the Open University offers flexibility that can be helpful – with assignment dates, for example. But finding the extra time you need as a dyslexic student will call for planning and organization, and those are themselves things that many dyslexic people find difficult. Try Activity 2 – it may help. Discussing your chart at the beginning of your course might be a good way to enable your tutor to appreciate some of your difficulties.

Activity 2
Finding time

The chart is divided into slots of one hour. Shade in one colour all the hours when you have work or other commitments. In another colour, shade in any travelling time. Don't use a dark colour for this – you might be able to use some of that time for reading or thinking. Shade in any regular leisure activities that you hope you can continue.

Now think about your study time. The average time for a 60-point course is 16 hours a week. It may take you longer, perhaps as much as double, so do allow for that. Shade a realistic number of hours in another colour. Look at these hours again later in your course, and adjust them if necessary.

With a bit of luck you'll have enough time left to spend with family and friends. Try to allow yourself some time off from study.

	Mon	Tues	Wed	Thurs	Fri	Sat	Sun
7am							
8							
9							
10							
11							
12							
1pm							
2							
3							
4							
5							
6							
7							
8							
9							
10							
11							
12							

Colour key

Work*	Travel	Time off	Study

* Paid or voluntary, or other fixed commitments

2.4 Choosing courses

All the evidence suggests that choosing the right course is the most important key to success in study. For all students that choice includes decisions such as:

Interest   It's a good idea to choose courses that will not be totally unfamiliar to you – where you already have some knowledge or experience of the subject. The chances are that if you're interested in a subject you will have done some reading and will have some idea of what studying it at university level will mean. Without real interest in the subject it's hard to keep going.

Long-term goals   Are you choosing a course because you just want to study the subject, or have you a longer-term goal for which you'll be choosing a series of courses, perhaps to qualify for a particular job? If you're not sure about this, it's worth asking yourself whether the course is to give you a general qualification, or something more specific, or whether you're doing it for personal satisfaction and interest.

Suitability   Many Open University courses have a great deal of reading material, which is likely to be especially demanding for dyslexic students. The good thing is that the courses are carefully written, at undergraduate level, and they contain all the material you need. There's no need to spend ages looking for materials in the library (which some dyslexic students find particularly difficult), and because the courses are designed for independent learning they are very carefully structured, with explanations, guides to working through the materials, practice questions and study tips throughout. They may also suggest the time that should be allocated to different study tasks. This is all helpful to a dyslexic student who finds organization a struggle.

On the other hand, such reliance on written materials can be particularly difficult for students whose learning style is less visual and who feel they learn best by listening and interacting in person. The Open University will provide recordings of most printed course material, which could help you.

At a more traditional higher education institution the very range of lectures and seminars can be a daunting feat of organization for some students (finding the right rooms, the right books, coping with the different styles of the lecturers, unclear verbal instructions and so on); for others the different interactions, discussions and varied learning contexts offer a supportive structure of daily activity and encouragement.

Being an Open University student can seem rather solitary and there's no doubt that you do most of the learning on your own. New technology means that if you're lucky enough to have a computer you can interact with other students in e-mail conference groups, and it can help with the business of writing and note-taking as well.

Time   All students say that 'finding the time' is the single greatest problem. Adult dyslexic students, trying to combine study with family and work commitments, may have to put more effort than others into meeting the constant and varied demands of the workplace. Add to that busy schedule the reading and essay-writing that are estimated to take an average student some 12–16 hours for a 60-point course and you can see why it's so important to work out your time and the demands of the course you're considering. As we have seen, dyslexic students are often very creative and highly intelligent but may need to allow twice as much time for their studies. While 12 hours a week may be possible, 24 may not.

Later on we discuss strategies for organization and note-taking that can reduce the reading time a little, but it should not be underestimated. It might be sensible to take a 30-point course and work under more reasonable pressure, even if it takes you longer to complete your degree, diploma or certificate.

Exams   Finally, it's worth considering the almost inevitable examination. This is part of the assessment for most, though not all, Open University courses. One student may be delighted at a multiple-choice format (no essay-writing), but another may be horrified at having to rely on less than perfect visual skills to find and tick the right boxes. If you can provide written evidence of your dyslexia, you can have appropriate arrangements for your exam such as extra time, a recorded question paper, or use of a computer or scribe.

2.4.1 A checklist to help you make your choice

Things to look for are:

- How much reading you'll have to do.
- Whether you have some familiarity with the area the course covers.
- How reading materials are presented.
- Whether there are recordings of printed material.
- How many assignments there are.

- Whether you'll need to use a computer.
- How many tutorials are offered.
- The nature of the examination.

As you consider possible courses, look for the particular features that will suit you. Some courses offer 'taster packs', materials selected from the course that give you an idea of the level and content. Open University Regional Centres have complete sets of materials from all the University's courses. You can look through them at your leisure and think about whether the design of the materials will suit your learning style (more about that in the next section). All the regions have advisory staff who can discuss course choice with you, and once you've registered for a course there are often workshops and materials to support your study.

Many dyslexic students think visually, spatially and holistically because they can visualize a whole system and see how it all fits together. If you think in that way you may find that courses in design, engineering and science particularly suit your talents.

2.5 Learning styles

No one person learns in exactly the same way as another. We do, however, fall into overlapping groups of learning styles, and it's very useful to be aware of your own group. It's particularly important if you're dyslexic. To understand how you learn and to know something about your preferred learning style is to recognize an area of strength.

We learn through our senses: by seeing, hearing, doing, touching, smelling. The last three are usually grouped together as 'kinaesthetic' or 'tactile' learning. A multisensory learner will use the senses equally, or use them all across the various kinds of learning. Most of us use one or two of the senses more effectively than the others.

2.5.1 Do you know how you learn?

Think about how you do things. When you recall things, do you have a vivid picture in your mind's eye? Then maybe you are a visual learner. Do you link memories more with sounds, music? If so, you may learn better by hearing things. Do you remember things you've done rather than things you've read or heard? If so, you might be a tactile or kinaesthetic learner.

There are various questionnaires you can use to decide which are your preferred learning styles and strengths. Try the one in Activity 3 at the end of this book. It might be helpful to discuss some of your answers with someone who knows you well.

2.5.2 *The dyslexic learning style*

As well as knowing something about the learning styles based on your senses, you'll find it useful to understand the *dyslexic learning style.*

Because the dyslexic brain tends to have a more developed right side, the side that deals with patterns and spatial awareness, you may have a tendency to be a holistic rather than a linear thinker – you work better from an overall picture than from a step-by-step (linear) process. You may be intuitive rather than deductive, perhaps reaching conclusions without knowing how or why. You may remember things in patterns instead of sequences. In fact you probably have difficulty remembering sequences such as the alphabet or telephone numbers. This may lead you to remember things by making connections that aren't apparent to other people. Your spatial awareness – ability to know how things might look from any direction – may be particularly good.

Take some time to reflect on your learning strengths. Activity 4 (at the end of this book) will start you off, and you can pin the chart up somewhere to remind you of these strengths. How many of the right-brained strengths have you got? Do you use them effectively?

> *You might like to make a list of particular concerns you have about your studies, as well as making yourself aware of your own learning style, so that you can talk them through with an adviser, or with your tutor once you are registered for a course.*

Famous dyslexics   Albert Einstein.   Leonardo da Vinci

3.1 Finding your own approach

This section is a collection of study strategies and ideas that students have tried and found helpful. Some of them may suit you better than others, so it's probably a good idea to read through them first and mark the ones that look most useful. Then try them out, adapting them to suit yourself.

Having a clear idea of which parts of studying you find most difficult will help you to select your strategies, so you might like to try Activity 5 first. If you prefer to work more visually, you can do the activity with the 'mindmap' that follows the list. Mindmapping is a visual, non-linear method of note-making, particularly suited to people who think holistically or visually rather than linearly.

Activity 5
Your study difficulties

Look at each topic in the list. In the box alongside the topic, write down what you find most difficult about it (or ask a friend or partner to write it for you). Beside *Reading*, for example, you might just write 'it takes me ages to read anything', or 'I keep losing my place'.

If you have difficulties with things that aren't on the list, add them, with your comments, in the empty boxes at the bottom.

Writing	
Reading	
Taking notes	
Spelling	
Proofreading	
Organizing materials	

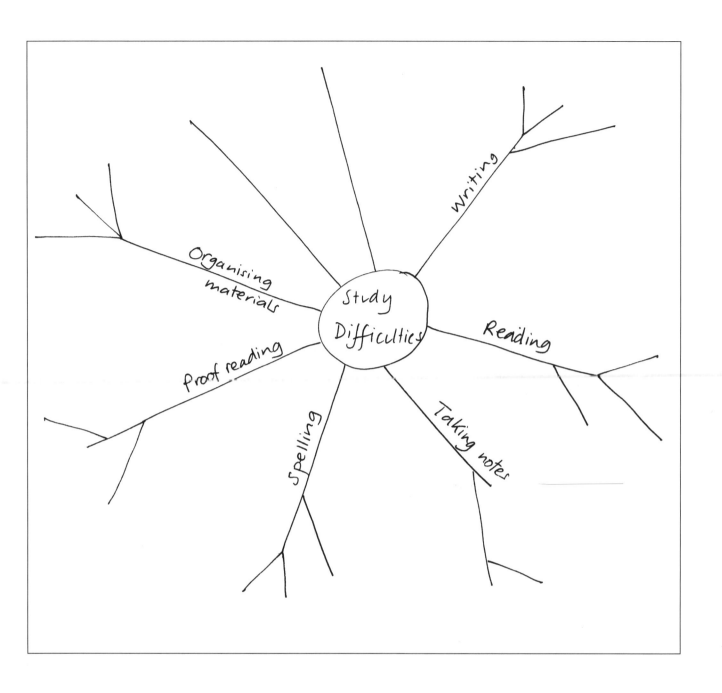

3.2 Getting organized

The desire to improve organizational skills usually stems from necessity. So take a look at your own circumstances and, if you feel that your life as a student would be improved by better organization, read on. Otherwise, come back to this section when you need to. Here are some questions to reflect on:

- Do you spend a lot of time looking for things you've lost?
- Do you forget appointments?
- Are you late for things more often than not?
- Do you run out of time?

If your answer to any of these questions is 'yes', you probably need to consider some strategies for planning and organizing your studies.

3.2.1 Strategies for organization

You don't have to be super-organized to study effectively. It's quite OK to be surrounded by apparent chaos, so long as it doesn't interfere with what you want to achieve. Many people feel more comfortable with chaos than with clinical tidiness.

We all have our own way of doing things, so no one can tell you how to organize yourself. We can only give you a few ideas to think about or to adapt. You almost certainly use some organizational strategies already, so try Activity 6 to help you to recognize what they are.

Activity 6
Your organizational strategies

Think of an occasion when you had to meet a deadline (writing a report for a meeting, making a wedding cake, getting the car ready for its MOT ...). Jot down your answers to the following questions:

What method(s) did you use to ensure that you met the deadline?

What materials did you use?

Who else was involved and how did you make sure that they did their part?

Did you meet the deadline? If not, what went wrong?

What would you do next time to make things work better?

Now think about how you organize your paperwork (your correspondence, your bills, your recipes …).

What do you use for filing? Shoe box, ringbinder, heap, what?

What order do you put things in? Date, alphabetical, topic, what?

How easy is it to find what you want?

Could other people find things?

How could you improve your system?

The activity has probably shown you that you do already use planning and organizational strategies. You might also be able to see where you could improve things.

3.2.2 Organizing your studies

First you'll need to think about the space you're going to use for your studies. Then you'll need to make some decisions about organizing the materials and equipment. Finally, you should think about the planning and organization of particular tasks.

Your study area should be a place where

- You can leave things where they won't be moved by you or anyone else.
- There's as little distraction as possible (noise, windows to gaze out of, and so on).
- It's warm in winter and cool in summer.
- There's ample space for worktop, filing, shelves, noticeboard etc.

- You can put up a large wall calendar, with colour-coded stickers for assignment dates, tutorials, exams and so on.

Your materials will come in all shapes and sizes, and there'll be a lot. One way to make them more manageable is by colour coding. Put a green label or small sticker on everything to do with history, for example, a red one on everything to do with literature and so on. If folders, books, notes, file cards, cassettes are all marked in this way, you can easily find the materials you need for the task in hand.

Your information – everything you need to learn and remember – will also be much more manageable if you pick out the important things and make them easy to find.

- You could make a list of key words and ideas; put them on a piece of card that will serve as a bookmark, or in a small address book, making a short specialist subject dictionary. You could deal in a similar way with more general phrases and instructions that crop up regularly, such as 'define', 'compare', 'contrast'.
- Expanding on the collection of key words, you could keep a colour-coded glossary card for each subject or topic. List important names, theories, vocabulary, formulae, and keep the card handy.
- To record information in more detail, use similar colour-coded cards and put a summary of a theory, experiment, idea on each one. Stack the cards by subject in a shoe box or card index box.

All these bookmarks, glossary cards and index cards will help you with spelling and vocabulary, and will be a useful aid when

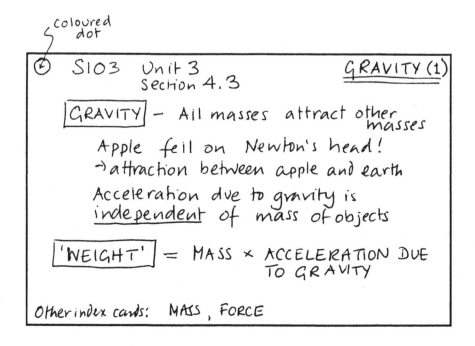

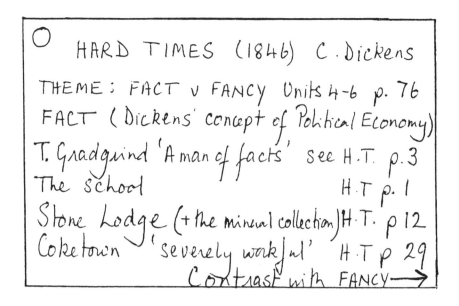

HARD TIMES (1846) C. Dickens

THEME: FACT v FANCY Units 4-6 p. 76

FACT (Dickens' concept of Political Economy)

T. Gradgrind 'A man of facts' see H.T. p.3

The school   H.T p. 1

Stone Lodge (+ the mineral collection) H.T. p 12

Coketown 'severely workful'   H.T p 29

Contrast with FANCY→

you write assignments or do revision.

3.3 Strategies to help with general study skills

3.3.1 Reading

Reading is a complicated activity that varies enormously according to what you're reading and why. Much of the reading for study introduces new ideas and new vocabulary.

If you have visual difficulties with print, try the coloured overlays we suggested in section 2.2. You might find that it's also helpful to enlarge the print, perhaps by photo-enlarging, using magnifying sheets, or electronically reformatting your text.

Before you start your reading you could ask your tutor to suggest the parts of the text that are essential, so that you can concentrate on those first. To get the most out of your reading, make it as active as possible:

- Make it as multisensory as you can. Read it out aloud, read it on to a tape and play it back while you follow the text.

- Stop frequently, perhaps at the end of each chunk or paragraph, and jot down a key word or phrase that sums up what you've just read.

- Ask yourself questions about what you've just read – what is the main point, what is being described?

- Take a brief break at the end of a page or section, to think about it and perhaps highlight or put a mark in the margin against the key idea.

- Make a large bookmark and write key definitions and key

concepts on it, to save time looking things up as you go along.

■ Always mark the spot you've reached in the text and write down a couple of phrases that summarize the last thing you read. When you return, you'll be able to pick up the text much more effectively.

3.3.2 Handwriting

The main thing that distinguishes adults' handwriting from children's is speed. As the writing speeds up, the joining of letters flows more easily. If you're copying very slowly and carefully, trying to reproduce the letters exactly, it's hard to keep the flow. A few suggestions:

■ Try different kinds of pen (biro, fibre-tip etc.) and experiment with colours to find the sort that suits you best.

■ If you find it hard to keep the size and shape of the letters regular, look for a basic book on handwriting. And if you practise with phrases that you want to learn anyway, you'll be helping your studies at the same time.

■ If correcting erratic spelling slows you down, write as freely as you can and then go back and correct.

A word-processor will, of course, spare you the difficulties of handwriting, and can prevent spelling errors as well. More about this in section 5.

3.3.3 Spelling

Your difficulty with spelling may be that you don't automatically make generalizations, so you have to learn each word individually. You may forget a spelling from one sentence to the next, so that you're always having to look it up. Spelling is one of the biggest worries, partly because of memories of school: the embarrassment of having to spell out loud or write on the blackboard. Most of us can remember the awful spelling tests and a row of red crosses against the words we were supposed to learn each week.

It's not always essential to spell with complete accuracy, unless a wrong spelling changes your meaning ('nitrate' for 'nitrite', for example). You won't necessarily be penalized for spelling errors in your course work. Ask your tutor what level of accuracy is acceptable, and discuss the most helpful way of having your mistakes pointed out.

Some strategies that can help with spelling:

- Learn some spelling rules that help you to avoid the mistakes you tend to make.

- Draw pictures to help imprint a spelling on your mind.

- Use mnemonics (a rhyme, a pun, anything that helps you to remember) to remind you of difficult spellings.

- Write words you use regularly on large pieces of paper with bright-coloured pens, and stick them up around the house.

- Write key words on cards that you can keep with you.

- Make a bookmark on stiff paper or card, and write key words on it.

- Collect words you want to learn in an address book. Keep it in a pocket and refer to it when you have a spare minute.

- Try using a spelling workbook or spelling dictionary. Some are suggested in section 7.1.3, page 69.

- Use a spellchecker, hand-held or on a computer. More about these in section 5, pages 57 and 59.

- If you have trouble looking words up in dictionaries and other reference books that are arranged in alphabetical order, try an alphabet arc.

    You can copy the arc on to a postcard and carry it with you. Some people like to cut it out and fold it along the lines into quadrants. It makes looking things up quicker and more accurate, and you won't have to start from the beginning of the alphabet for each word.

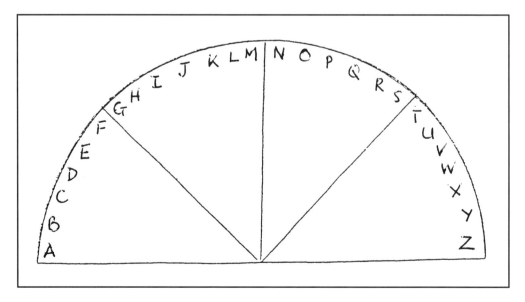

Alphabet arc

3.3.4 Taking notes

You'll take more effective notes if you're clear in your mind about what they're for, and about what sort of notes work well for you. We recommend the Open University Student Toolkit no. 4 *Reading and Note-taking*; ask your Regional Centre for a copy.

Activity 7
What are notes for?

Try making a list or a mindmap to reflect on this.

An example is shown at the end of Activity 5 in section 3.1. See also Student Toolkit 4 *Reading and Note-taking*, pages 28–9.

Activity 8
Your own notes

Discuss your ideas with a group, or make a rough list or mindmap:

The best thing about my notes ...

The worst thing about my notes ...

Activity 8
What kind of notes?

Look at these example of notes:

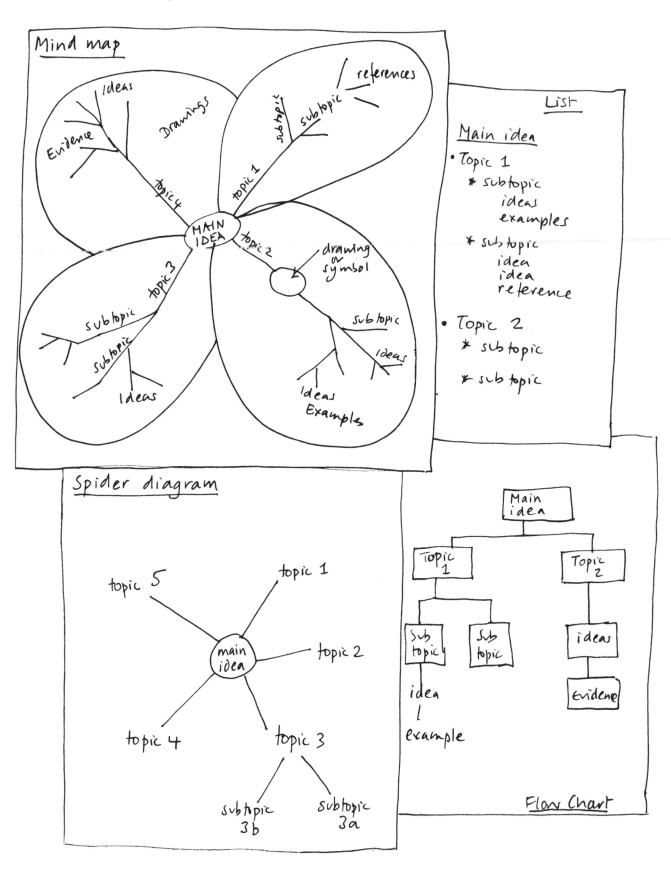

Mind map

Spider diagram

List

Flow Chart

Jot down any thoughts and ideas about what's good and what's bad. Add any points about what might work for you.

We sometimes think that we take notes so that we'll have a written record of something we've read. But there are other kinds of notes too. You might write out a shopping list, or instructions for finding your way somewhere. You may throw notes away when they've served their purpose. You might write notes that help you to make links in your head between ideas. Making notes helps you to concentrate and forces you to prioritize the important points. Notes of that kind are not intended as a record, but are a means of clarifying your thoughts. So taking notes can help you in several ways:

- Concentrating – the process of thinking and writing can help you to focus your attention and so to learn more effectively.

- Remembering – writing something down can help you to remember it. You can also refer back to it to check your memory.

- Understanding – making rough notes or a diagram can help you to 'unpack' complex parts of your reading material.

- Keeping a record – of talks, tutorials, broadcasts, things you need to do.

- Summarizing – the key points of procedures, course units and so on. Try choosing any passage from a text and writing down five points made in it. Then try linking them in continuous prose, for writing practice. This may be something that a tutor can help you with in an additional session.

- Reordering or organizing materials in a way that suits your learning style and picks out the things you need to learn.

- Highlighting key points or ideas so that you can refer to them later.

- Planning. Notes are a good way to start off your ideas for an assignment.

If you work better visually or spatially rather than in writing, you can make graphic 'notes': flow charts, block designs, family trees, spider plans or other forms of mindmap. There are some good examples in *The Study Skills Handbook* – see page 70.

3.3.5 Writing and checking essays

It's been suggested that there are two aspects of writing: composition and transcription. Composition is the gathering of ideas, selecting words and getting it all on paper in fluent sentences and paragraphs. Transcription is the physical act of writing legibly, with correct spelling and punctuation.

Composition	Transcription
Getting ideas	Physical act of writing
Selecting words	Correct spelling
Grammar	Correct punctuation
Sentence structure	Legibility Paragraphs

Transcription can be tiring. Writing is always slower than the thought process, and gets untidier and less accurate as you try to speed up. So it's sensible to separate transcription from composition. Get your ideas sorted out first. Then, when you've got a rough draft to work from, you can concentrate on the act of writing.

Composition   Methodical drafting will improve the quality of your written work. The chart below suggests a general approach:

Drafting

Stage	Tasks	Objectives
Before drafting	Gather all *relevant* information (index cards, notes etc.).	Getting ideas
	Produce an overview of all topics required (e.g. spider plan, mindmap, list).	Selecting words
	Group ideas and topics together (e.g. using coloured highlighters).	Basic paragraph structure
Drafting	Take each topic separately. Write a list of relevant points, using short sentences.	Basic sentences
Discuss draft	Read and discuss with your tutor or another student, for *content* and *structure*. Mark comments in pencil.	Content and structure
Second draft	Make second draft, incorporating comments.	Content, structure and grammar

Some strategies to help with composition:

- When planning your work, divide your ideas into small sections. Put each new section on a different piece of paper.

- Try to develop 'topic' sentences to put at the head of each section. Then you can add further examples and illustrations of the point you're making.

- Try making a mindmap or diagram to get your ideas down on paper without worrying about sentences.

- You might find that dictating into a tape-recorder allows you to think and express your ideas without having to deal with the mechanics of writing.

- Try writing short numbered sentences to begin with, each covering one point. Ideas can be joined by using link words such as 'and', 'but', 'however'.

- Look at examples of essays and break them down into their different parts (introduction, paragraph one about x, paragraph two about y etc.). Use these structures for your essay.

- Discuss your rough draft with other students or your tutor. Consider things like giving emphasis to your main points, linking paragraphs, use of references and quotations.

- When your work has been marked, discussion with other students can give you more ideas about good construction and other aspects of composition.

If you use a computer you might consider trying the software packages that help you to organize your ideas. We suggest a few to look at in section 5.6 on page 60.

Transcription　When you're satisfied with the content and structure, read through your draft to check spelling, punctuation and legibility. It can be very difficult to spot your own errors, especially if dyslexia affects your visual perception. Read your work several times over, and concentrate on something different each time: spelling, paragraphing, punctuation. Some other suggestions that might help you to pick up mistakes:

- Read your essay backwards, from the end to the beginning, word by word. You'll spot many of your mistakes, and notice words you're not sure of.

- Correct errors *immediately*. Note in the margin any words you think you might have spelt wrongly. Then ask someone, or use a dictionary, to correct those.

- Read the essay from the beginning and look for errors related to your particular difficulties – omitted words, wrong punctuation, grammar.

- Try reading the work on to a tape and playing it back. You're likely to notice any passages that don't make sense.

- Use the proofreading checklist in Appendix 1.

Word-processors and other technology can be particularly helpful with the transcription aspect of writing essays. If you're interested, look at section 5.3 (page 56).

3.3.6 *Multiple-choice questions*

Multiple-choice questions are now widely used. The Open University's computer-marked assignments, for example, consist entirely of multiple-choice questions. They require careful reading, and it's easy to be misled by the form of the question even if you have a good understanding of the subject. If you have difficulties with reading, try recording the questions and listening to them as you look at the printed text.

Often you're asked to write your answers on a special form. This can also be troublesome if you're dyslexic. If it puts you at a disadvantage you should ask someone to help you with the form. In extreme cases you might be allowed to submit the assignment in a different way.

3.3.7 *Tutorials*

Unlike lectures, tutorials don't usually present a section of the course or discuss a single topic. Instead, they explore important areas of the subject, issues raised by an assignment question, or concepts that students find particularly challenging.

No one finds it easy to listen, take part in the discussion, take notes and look up references all at the same time. If you're dyslexic you can spend far too long trying to find the passage or to write something down while the discussion carries on without you. Some suggestions that might help with this and with other aspects of tutorials:

- In advance of the tutorial, ask what passages or sections of the course the tutor is likely to be looking at. Then you can prepare those in advance, and perhaps mark the key words, underline things you want to remember, and note any questions you want to ask.

- Ask the tutor to put an outline of the topics on the board, and to provide handouts. You might prefer to do this in an individual discussion early in the course, but the extra clarity, examples and structure will help everyone else as well.

- Take a small tape-recorder, so that you can concentrate on listening and take notes later from the recording. You needn't record the whole tutorial (it would take a long time to listen to), just appropriate parts.

- Try just jotting down short phrases, leaving a space of a few lines in between them. Then fill them in as you listen to your recording. Your outline might look something like this:

Tutorial one – block one

Social values

Treatment of women/Old people/Children

Education see page 31

- Other students will be taking notes, so ask someone for a copy and adapt them to suit yourself.

After the first tutorial take ten minutes to reflect on what went on, while it's still fresh in your mind. What would have helped you to get even more out of it? Spend another five minutes highlighting from your notes the points you feel were the ones to expand later.

Don't worry too much about taking detailed notes in tutorials. All the information is in your course materials. Just note anything that makes things clearer to you.

Individual sessions with your tutor can be very productive. Half an hour before or after a tutorial can help, but a special session gives you time to ask about things you're struggling with and to discuss your own written work. The more you prepare, the more useful the session will be. Even a single session can make all the difference. Some Open University students may have two or three special sessions during a course, arranged with the tutor and the Regional Centre.

3.4 Strategies to help with particular subjects

3.4.1 Music

Many dyslexic students are very musical and can carry a tune or a rhythm in their heads easily. Often, when they appear to be playing from a sheet of music, they are in fact playing from memory. Reading music can be particularly challenging to dyslexic people because it uses its own set of names and symbols, and because the same shape in a different position represents a different note. All this on top of the complex physical activity of pressing, bowing, blowing and fingers doing different things at the same time. A few suggestions for learning to read music:

■ Coloured overlays can counteract visual distortion, just as they do with print.

■ Try writing the names of the notes on the keyboard, or on a bookmark.

■ Mnemonics can be very helpful (FACE for the four spaces in the treble clef, for example).

3.4.2 Languages

Learning a new language means a lot of new vocabulary, made even more difficult by unfamiliar pronunciation. It helps to learn something of the structure of the language, the 'rules' that aid learning as spelling rules do in your first language. If you know, for example, that verbs end in -ir, -er or -re, that narrows the possibilities. You're not simply trying to remember the spelling but using your logic and your long-term memory of patterns. Some other suggestions:

■ Make your learning visually arresting and colourful. Use pictures, however simple, with phrases in balloons, or diagrams with labels to establish the link between a new word and a familiar object.

■ Make your learning multisensory. Try the 'look, cover, check' method: say the word as you hear it, copy it down saying it aloud as you do so, cover the word up and write it again, check it.

■ Use repetition – chant it, speak it into a tape recorder or to a friend. Speak it out in an exaggerated way until the repetition takes root.

■ Learn model phrases or sentences.

- Practise adapting the model by changing the verb ('j'aime les fruits', 'je déteste les fruits') or some other part ('je veux visiter les grandes villes', 'je veux visiter les chateaux').

- Put key words on a card each, then collect more words on the same theme.

3.4.3 Maths

About 60 per cent of dyslexic people have some difficulties with maths. The difficulties can be to do with:

- *Decoding* the numbers, letters and symbols.

- Understanding and remembering the *language* of maths, science and technology.

When you look at numbers, letters and symbols your brain has to decide what they mean. This decoding is done in the working memory, and is in most people a fast and automatic process. Dyslexia can both slow down the process and cause errors, such as mistaking 6 for 9. This kind of difficulty tends to affect arithmetic. Many people who say that they're 'no good at maths' really mean that they have trouble with arithmetic. And being slower than other people doesn't mean you're less intelligent!

Because many dyslexic people have a 'right-brained' learning style, see things holistically and intuitively, they can be adept at making connections and seeing patterns. So those who find ways to overcome the decoding and language difficulties are likely to enjoy and be good at maths.

Some strategies for decoding and dealing with numbers and formulae:

Say it out loud, tracking each figure with your finger as you go. Using your visual and auditory senses, and to some extent your touch as well, can straighten out numbers that bewilder the eye alone: 1066, for example, is easily confused with 1099, 1660, 1990, 6601.

Chunk and say If you need to remember a number the safest way is to write it down, saying it aloud to make sure that you've written it correctly. But another way to remember is to 'chunk' it. Instead of remembering eleven digits for a telephone number, break it into five or six numbers and remember those. Instead of 01908 274066, remember that all British numbers start with zero, then memorize *Nineteen, Oh eight, Twenty-seven, Forty, Sixty-six*.

You can use a similar strategy for more complex expressions such as the velocity of light, 2.997925×10^8 ms^{-1}. To remember it to six decimal places, chunk it into *Two point, Ninety-nine, Seventy-nine, Twenty-five, Times ten to the eight*, or into *Two point nine, Nine seven nine, Two five, Times ten to the eighth, Metres per second*. It may be that for most purposes you need recall the value only approximately, and look it up if you want it precisely. Then you need remember only 3×10^8 ms^{-1}.

Chanting the chunks to a familiar tune or a rhythm can help. Tunes like the *Can-Can* are surprisingly adaptable!

Remembering by understanding   Understanding the meaning of formulae and equations will help you both to remember and to use them. Try translating them into words. Einstein's famous formula $e=mc^2$, for example:

energy	e
equals	=
mass	m
times	
the square of the velocity of light	c^2

If difficulties with reading affect your comprehension and so get in the way of solving mathematical problems, adapt some of the strategies you use for non-mathematical reading and writing:

Make a specialist dictionary   Whenever you meet a new technical word, or one you can't remember, write it down. Underneath, write the definition, and the sentence, phrase or formula where you first saw it. You might add associated words, a diagram or sketch, and the relevant mathematical symbol (÷, % or Σ, for example). Use coloured pens or highlighters to make it memorable. Make your dictionary in a small notebook that you keep with you, or on index cards, keeping a supply of blanks handy. Arrange your words in the way that suits you best – it doesn't have to be in alphabetical order. Do it in topic order, or by sound, for example.

Concrete example   Instead of trying to think of it in abstract terms, link your word or idea to a real example. Visualize that every time you meet the word. You could visualize 'ellipse' with the double L inside an ellipse, for example. That will help you to remember how to spell it, though people will know what you mean if you spell it with only one L. Technical words are often misspelt by non-dyslexic people too!

Chunk and chant   Chunk your word into groups of letters and chant them. For example, i-s...o-s...c-e-l...e-s.

Is your answer sensible?   Always ask yourself this. A simple example:

> You leave home at 10 am to visit a friend who lives 1000 km away. You hope to be able to keep up a speed of 100 km per hour, so you tell your friend to expect you at 11 am.
>
> Is that reasonable? No, it certainly isn't! The journey couldn't possibly take only 1 hour. You'll have to check your figures – you've probably made an error with all those noughts.

Multiplication tables

Multiplication tables can be difficult or impossible for dyslexic people to learn in the conventional way – by remembering sequences. There are other approaches that might suit your learning style better:

Recognizing patterns   Think of tables in terms of a pattern. All the multiplications up to 12 are in this square, twice, across and down. So you really need only half the square and to remember half the table:

	1	2	3	4	5	6	7	8	9	10	11	12
2	4	6	8	10	12	14	16	18	20	22	24	
3	6	9	12	15	18	21	24	27	30	33	36	
4	8	12	16	20	24	28	32	36	40	44	48	
5	10	15		25	30	35	40	45	50	55	60	
6	12	18			36	42	48	54	60	66	72	
7	14	21				49	56	63	70	77	84	
8	16	24	32	40	48	56	64	72	80	88	96	
9	18	27						81	90	99	108	
10	20	30							100	110	120	
11	22	33								121	132	
12	24	36									144	

To multiply the bold numbers in the top row by the bold numbers in the left-hand column, find the answer where the column and row cross. Follow the shaded row and column and you'll see that 7 x 8 is 56. Now check, in the same way, that 8 x 7 is also 56.

Activity 9
The multiplication square

Look at the patterns down the columns and across the rows of the square. As you go down the column headed 2, you're adding 2 to each number – you're counting in twos – 2, 4, 6, 8, etc. In the column headed 3 you're counting in threes, and so on. Now look at the row that starts with 2 and the one that starts with 3. They're the same as the columns that start with 2 and 3. There's a row identical to every column, so you can now complete the table. See how the numbers repeat themselves on either side of the shaded diagonal?

Using your hands   This *fast finger* method works for some people. You can use it only for numbers from 6 to 10, and you have to be able to multiply numbers below 6 in your head or in some other way.

Number the fingers on both hands from 6 to 10:

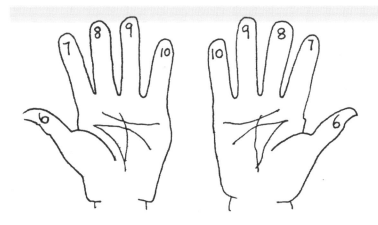

Example To multiply 8 by 9

Place your palms together but not touching

Put the tip of the finger marked 8 of one hand to touch the tip of the finger marked 9 on the other hand

Count the fingers and thumbs from your thumbs up to and including the two fingers that are touching – 7. This is the number of tens – 70.

Count the remaining fingers on one hand and multiply it by the number of remaining fingers on the other – two fingers left on one hand and one on the other: 2 x 1 = 2. These are the units.

Put the tens and units together to get 72.

8 x 9 = 72 ✓

Now try it with 6 x 7:

Palms facing

Thumb 6 to finger 7 of other hand

3 tens = 30

3 x 4 = 12

30 + 12 = 42

6 x 7 = 42 ✓

With practice you can check your multiplication very quickly.

> *Discover your own learning style.*
> *Make learning multisensory – see it, feel it, hear it.*
> *Make it all active.*

SECTION 4
REVISION AND EXAMS

4.1 Thinking about revision and exams

Revision should begin at the start of your course, so don't leave this section until a week before the exam! We hope that you'll be able to find some revision and exam strategies here to suit you. You can work through various ideas on your own or with your tutor. We suggest that you have at least one session on exams with your course tutor or with a dyslexia adviser. Regular practice of techniques for answering examination questions, throughout your course, would be useful.

Many people find exams difficult and stressful, but dyslexia can compound the difficulties:

Cause of difficulty	Possible solutions
Timed conditions can affect reading, writing, spelling and comprehension	Extra time Use time carefully Plan
Memory	Memory strategies Understanding
Significant discrepancy between course work and exam performance	Appropriate exam facilities Anxiety strategies

Good planning and organization are very helpful with revision, and essential for doing yourself justice in the exam. Activity 10 will help you to reflect on the way you have planned your revision in the past. Try it now, and then read on.

Activity 10
Thinking about your exam

Remember what approaches you've taken in the past, and jot down answers to these questions:

When do you normally start to revise for the exam?

Was this too early or too late?

Do exams make you feel very anxious, so that your anxiety affects your performance?

Do you do anything beforehand to minimize those effects?

Do you make a revision plan? If so, what information do you use to help you plan?

4.2 How do you memorize?

How you remember things will depend on your learning style, so make sure that you know how you learn best. If you haven't already done so:

- Try Activity 3 (in Appendix 2 at the end of this book) to identify which of the senses you use most effectively.

- Try Activity 4 (at the end of the book) to see whether your strengths are predominantly right-brained or left-brained.

Some basic facts about memory:

- Your understanding will increase over a long period of study, but the ability to remember decreases. Find what your optimum learning period is and take short breaks in between. We suggest trying study periods of 20 to 40 minutes, with breaks of 3 to 10 minutes. Experiment to find your best pattern. Remember that it can vary, depending on your physical and mental state, the time of day and even the weather.

- The greatest memory loss is within 24 hours of learning something, so review your learning within that time. If you study during the evening, go over the materials on your way to work the next day. A 5 or 10-minute review then will be more useful than a longer one later. Build review into your study plan. When revision begins in earnest, say 6 to 8 weeks before the exam, you'll be able to remember more.

- Things can be committed to memory more easily if they are:

Brief

Clear

Understood

Multisensory

Repeated

Linked or sequential (recall one thing and others will follow)

- Recall tends to get progressively worse during an exam, unless the mind is given brief rests.

While you're learning:

- Avoid distractions, especially visual ones. Background music of the right kind can be helpful in filtering out sudden distracting sounds.

- Be interested. It's very difficult to learn things that you don't find interesting.

- Be active. Say it, write it, imagine it, draw it, act it out.

- Use repetition or chanting.

- Invent and use mnemonics.

4.3 Paving the way for revision

From the beginning of your course you should try to identify the concepts that you need to learn. Then you can extract them and put them into a form that *you* can best learn from. Some suggestions:

- Make notes that are visual.

- Condense the information as much as you can. Memorize the points that will trigger your recall of other facts.

- Put all your condensed notes about one topic on one page.
- Use colour to highlight – a different colour for each topic, for example.
- Make big posters for each topic, using colour and other visual clues. Pin them up where you can look at them frequently.
- Make diagrams and charts.
- Record facts and information on tape, to listen to in the car or out walking.

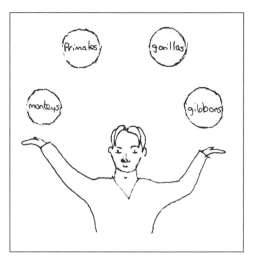

The object of these strategies is to minimize the amount you need to read when you revise. You may devise other methods or use a mixture of some of these. Try different ideas and use what works best for you.

4.4 Revision activities throughout the course

Revision should be a continuous process. If you've prepared for revision in the way that we've suggested, you'll be able to revise whenever you have a spare moment. Here are some ideas for revision activities. They include repeating, reciting and rewriting to help you to remember the information:

- Divide each revision session into short periods, with regular breaks.

- Self-test. At the end of each session test yourself without looking at the information, then check. Note the bits you couldn't recall and learn those.

- Quick review. After a break, look over the things you revised before the break. Then move on.

- Practise. Use old exam papers to practise on. It's never too soon to start doing this.

- Practise analysing each question and deciding what it means. Try the 'PTFE' (Process, Topic, Focus, Examples) approach explained in Activity 12 at the end of this section.

- Practise organizing your thoughts on a range of exam questions by quickly jotting down ideas as they come into your head – brainstorming. Then put them into groups of related ideas. Now put the groups into a logical order. Allow 5 to 10 minutes for this.

- Practise answering some whole questions. After brainstorming and ordering your ideas, practise writing your answer within the time limit for the question.

4.5 Planning revision sessions

The chart below suggests a structure you could follow for each topic you need to revise, incorporating the strategies we've described. You can adapt this plan to suit your needs. The first two stages should take place *during* your course, to spread the load and to ensure that you're regularly reviewing what you learn.

Ideally you should start the third stage no later than three weeks before the exam. Any later will leave too little time for proper revision, much more will affect your ordinary course work. You can use the chart in Activity 10 to help you plan your third stage.

Stage	Task	Timing
1 Preparing for revision	Prepare revision notes: Visual or auditory Condensed One side per topic Posters Charts Diagrams Mindmaps Be selective!	As soon as you have a good grasp of the concepts.
2 Revision activities	Without looking at your notes, jot down any key words, phrases, formulae that you can remember about the topic. Check them against your revision notes. Make corrections and additions, preferably in a different colour.	One or two weeks after stage 1 and at other odd times during the course. Reviewing what you've learnt should be a continuous process.
3 Final revision	Don't read anything new at this stage. Continue revision activities, but keep to a plan to cover as much of the course as you need to.	During the last few weeks before the exam.

When you get to this stage we have two pieces of advice:

- Don't try to learn anything that you haven't understood. It's probably too late.

- Don't spend time learning things you already know. This is why revision sessions should start with self-testing.

Activity 11
A revision timetable

The chart is to help you plan a 3-week revision period. Mornings, afternoons and evenings are each divided into 3 sessions. These are flexible – you may be able to fit in 4, or prefer only 2. Our 3-session plan assumes that you study for about an hour and take a 15-minute break between sessions.

Fill in your own times in the left-hand column. Then blank out all the times that you won't be able to study, because of work or other commitments.

Make a list of all the topics you need to revise, in order of priority. You may have to consider not revising some at all. If you're short of time, remember that you'll cope best with the topics you enjoy most, and scrap the ones you find most difficult. Make sure you include the topics that are central to the course. If you look at past papers, you'll see which topics come up again and again.

Now try fitting your topics into the chart – do it in pencil. You could see one subject right through in consecutive sessions, or you might prefer to start or finish each revision day with your favourite topic. It's up to you. You can change things as you go, but the benefit of the chart is that you can work through the course systematically, ticking off each topic as you go.

Week 1

Time	Mon	Tues	Wed	Thurs	Fri	Sat	Sun

Week 2

Time	Mon	Tues	Wed	Thurs	Fri	Sat	Sun

Week 3

Time	Mon	Tues	Wed	Thurs	Fri	Sat	Sun

4.6 The examination

4.6.1 Anxiety

Feeling anxious gets the adrenaline going, and that often improves performance. But over-anxiety can have the opposite effect. If this is a problem for you we recommend the Student Toolkit *Revision and Exams*, which has an excellent section on dealing with anxiety.

4.6.2 Exam conditions

Having the right conditions and facilities for your exam will help to relieve the additional stress that dyslexia can cause. It isn't cheating to have them. Extra time is essential if your reading or writing is slow, and it will give you time to use your planning strategies too. You may also need short rest breaks.

If getting things down on paper is laborious, or if your handwriting becomes illegible under pressure, you can consider dictating your answers or using a word-processor. If you feel that you can't do yourself justice unless you use a word-processor, be sure that you know exactly how to save your answers to disk and print them out. Technology going wrong will only add to the stress. If in doubt, ask to dictate to a scribe (amanuensis).

For most subjects spelling won't matter so long as words are recognizable. But if your spelling deteriorates badly under pressure, ask your Regional Centre about the use of spellcheckers, spelling books or a scribe in exams.

You might want to use coloured overlays, or to have the exam questions printed on coloured paper or in large print, or to have recordings of the questions as well as the printed paper. Ask for what you need well in advance, so that there's time for it to be set up. Seek advice, and try to strike a balance that leaves you under enough pressure to get that adrenaline going.

It's important to practise exam techniques beforehand, using past papers if you can. It's also important to practise with your scribe, if you're going to have one.

4.6.3 Planning your time

Even if you're allowed extra time you'll be working to time limits. It's best to work out well beforehand how much time you should spend on each question or each part of the paper. You can use the specimen paper or past papers to apportion your time. Take a simple case: you have a 3-hour exam with 30 minutes extra time. You are required to answer 4 questions out of 8, each carrying 25 per cent of the marks. How long should you spend on each question?

Try working it out for yourself, then see if you agree with us.

We allowed ourselves 10 full minutes to read the paper through and decide which questions we would answer. We also decided to allow at least 10 minutes at the end to check through our answers. That leaves us 3 hours 10 minutes to divide between 4 questions. That means 47 minutes for each question, and 2 minutes over. We decided to spend 45 minutes on each question. The exam is to start at 2.00, so we'll start writing at about 2.10 and stop the first question at 2.55, and so on.

Was your plan similar to ours?

A couple more ideas to help with time:

- Put your watch or a small clock on your table, and stick to the times you've worked out.

- Start each answer on a fresh page in the answer book, leaving some space after each answer in case you want to add something later.

4.6.4 The questions

Exam questions may be

Essays

Structured questions with many parts

Questions that require short answers, notes or diagrams

Multiple choice

One way to analyse and decode exam questions is suggested here. If you think it might suit you, practise using it on old exam papers so that you're comfortable with it before you take your exam.

Activity 12
Decoding questions: the PTFE approach
Process, Topic, Focus, Examples

If you can identify what the examiner is asking you to do, you are well on the way to answering the question.

This is a good activity to work on with your tutor.

P is for process word

Somewhere in the question you'll find a process word or a phrase that suggests a process. Highlight it in colour. Examples of process words and phrases are:

The process words	How to begin
Explain..... How...? In what way......? Why......?	Imagine you're explaining the topic to a fellow student
What is the difference..... Contrast....	Make a list for each topic
Assess.....	
Evaluate....	
Estimate the effects.....	

You can use the spaces to add other process words you come across. If you're not sure what a word is asking you to do, discuss it with your tutor, then fill in the *How to begin column*.

T is for Topic

The question will be about a particular topic. Examples could be: local government in the 1960s, mitosis, eradication of smallpox, Eliza Doolittle. Use another colour to highlight the topic.

F is for Focus

The question is unlikely to want you to write everything you know about the topic. There will be a focus. For example, it may want you to discuss the *relationship* between Eliza and Professor Higgins. Find the focus and highlight it in another colour.

You now have a good idea of what the examiner is asking you, and you have a colour-coded reminder to refer back to.

E is for Examples

Your answer will be enriched by examples and they will gain you extra marks. They will also add weight to your arguments. Often some marks are set aside specifically for examples.

Exams give an indication of your level of expertise in a particular subject.
They are not a test of you as a human being.

SECTION 5
HOW TECHNOLOGY CAN HELP

5.1 What's available?

A vast range of technological aids is now available, and more are appearing all the time. Some devices are sophisticated and expensive, others are surprisingly simple and cheap. Don't be tempted to rush out and buy everything. What works best for you will depend on the nature of your dyslexia and the demands of your course. Get some advice from your Regional Centre first, then try things out at a specialist centre. Keep a look out for new ideas, and for new ways of using old technology.

If you have to buy equipment, don't forget that much of it is likely to be useful to other members of your household too. Prices are coming down all the time, and you may find that there are funds that can help you with your expenses. You might be able to use Disabled Students' Allowances, for example. You have to have a recent formal assessment of your study needs to be eligible for these. Ask your Regional Centre if you want to know more about them.

It's very important to get proper training for any equipment that you acquire. You'd be surprised how much technology is lying around in homes and offices unused because people haven't had adequate training and so haven't even been able to get started. If you're completely unfamiliar with computers and information technology, we recommend that you get some basic information first. The British Dyslexia Association has a useful booklet called *IT for Dyslexic Adults: a Booklet for Beginners*, and there are many other introductory guides to be found in bookshops.

5.2 Help with reading

5.2.1 Electronic files

Many documents, including tutors' handouts, may be available as electronic files. With a computer you can adapt and use them to overcome some of your own dyslexic difficulties. You can:

- Change the typeface and the size of the letters. Some people also find that $1\frac{1}{2}$-line spacing makes text much easier to read.

- Change the colour of the letters and of the background.

- Copy extracts from the text into your own notes.

- Add your own notes to the text.

5.2.2 Speech output

With appropriate software, your computer can read the text out loud as it appears on the screen. You need a multimedia computer for this, or you might be able to upgrade an older model. The synthesized speech may not be easy on the ear, though these artificial voices are improving all the time.

Speech output can be useful in the same way as recorded course materials and talking books. You might be particularly glad of it if the materials you want aren't available as recordings. The spoken text can help you with:

- Comprehension and concentration.

- Pronunciation of new and unfamiliar words.

- Skim-reading.

- Proofreading your own work.

5.2.3 Scanners

If your course materials aren't available as electronic files, a scanner might be worth having. It's a hand-held or flat-bed device (something like a photocopier) that reads the text and converts it to a word-processed document. You can adapt and use that in all the ways we've already suggested. Scanners sometimes run into trouble when presented with unclear print, symbols or complex layouts.

5.2.4 Reading pen

A reading pen is a miniature scanner, about the size of a chunky pen. It has a synthesized voice and can be used with an ear-piece. It reads out individual words and can give their definitions, though it might not recognize some highly specialized words. Prices are still quite high, but are coming down.

There are similar devices for scanning bits of text – quotations and things you want to remember – so that you can load them into your computer.

5.3 Help with writing

Many dyslexic people are articulate and express themselves well verbally. Slow writing, lack of confidence with spelling or grammar and other difficulties can interfere with the flow of ideas. Technology can help by separating the 'transcription' skills from the 'composition' – the ideas and structure.

5.3.1 Word-processors

A word-processor will make the transcription aspect of writing much less laborious. You can set it up so that your text is as easy as possible for you to read, and you can use its features in the ways that suit you best. Place your screen where it will be free of reflections, and adjust its brightness and contrast. Some choices you can make:

■ The colour of the text and the background.

■ The shape and size of the letters. You can also use *Zoom* to make the 'page' on your screen whatever size you find easiest to work with.

■ Make your text left-justified (as in this book). Many dyslexic people find that this helps to overcome visual distortion.

■ Use the keyboard or the mouse, whichever you prefer.

■ Set up *Autocorrect* to correct errors you're particularly likely to make, and to complete words and phrases you type in frequently.

■ Put more control buttons on the toolbar, to save yourself hunting through the menus.

■ Use *Outline* so that you can see the structure of your document and change it easily.

■ Create a template if you're going to produce several documents of a similar kind.

■ Be sure to save your work frequently – every 5 minutes, if possible.

You might need someone to explain how to do these things. Consider taking a word-processing course if you don't feel confident about exploring the software for yourself.

5.3.2 Predictive software

Predictive software offers you a choice of words. When you type the first few letters of a word, a list of the words you use most commonly will be displayed. You click on the right one,

and it will be typed in for you. For example, if you type 'p, s, y'
you might get:

psychology
psychologist
psyche
psychiatry
psycho-analyst
psychotic

You can use speech output to read out the word you highlight,
and choose the right one by its sound. The more letters you
can type in, the more likely you are to get the word you want in
the selection. The software remembers how often and how
recently you've used the words it comes up with, and puts
them in order.

5.3.3 Spellcheckers and grammar checkers

Standard word-processing packages are giving more and
more help with spelling and grammar. Make sure that you're
using the features you already have before you consider
buying extra software. Some packages offer help with words
that are spelt differently but sound the same ('hear' and 'here')
by giving you an idea of the meaning. Some use grammar
rules to help you decide on the right word. More about
spellcheckers in 5.5.1 *Spelling*.

Some word-processing packages come with spelling and
grammar checks switched on, so that they highlight or even
correct your mistakes as you type. You may find that these
interruptions interfere with the flow of your ideas. You can alter
the default settings so that the checks are not automatically
on, then run them when you come to a natural break in your
writing. Make sure that your language setting is *UK English*;
the default setting is often *US English*.

5.3.4 Dictation

Dictating can remove many of the difficulties of 'transcription'.

Recording and transcribing   You could speak your ideas
into an audio-cassette recorder, then type them into your word-
processor like an audio-typist. Then you can use the word-
processor to correct and edit your text.

Voice recognition software   You talk straight at your computer, which transcribes your speech into word-processed text. You may have trouble if your speech isn't particularly clear or varies a lot. Whatever your speech is like, you'll need training, and so will your computer – it has to learn to recognize your voice. This may mean several hours of work. You'll probably need to weigh the inconveniences of the software against the degree of difficulty you have with the keyboard or with transcribing your ideas. Many voice recognition software packages are available at affordable prices. Get advice from a specialist, and buy the best you can afford. Before you buy anything, try it out.

5.4 Help with taking notes

Taking notes usually means doing several tasks at the same time – listening or reading, understanding, summarizing, writing. This is bad news if you're dyslexic, but technology can help.

5.4.1 Tape recorders, mini-disk and digital recorders

It's possible to record lectures or tutorials and make notes from your recordings. This may be a good idea occasionally, but is very time-consuming. For most occasions we recommend using a pocket memo recorder to make brief verbal notes.

Mini-disk and digital recorders are more expensive than tape or cassette recorders, but are more versatile. You can use them to dictate into voice recognition software when you're away from your computer. You might find that more convenient than lugging a laptop around with you.

5.4.2 Laptop computers

These are expensive but portable. You could use a laptop as your main computer. You can use word-processing software to type notes, and there is specialist software that produces mindmaps or flow diagrams.

5.4.3 Palmtops

These are very compact computers that you can hold in your hand. Notes that you make on them can be transferred to an ordinary computer and edited.

5.5 Help with individual words

You might want to check a spelling, check the meaning of a word, or find the right word to use. Dyslexic difficulties with reading, alphabetic order and so on can make using a dictionary laborious, if not impossible. There are technological aids that can help.

5.5.1 Spelling

The spellcheckers incorporated in word-processors are useful, but not infallible. They can't distinguish a misspelt word if the misspelling is itself a word. So if you mistyped 'boat' as 'beat' it would be happy with that. As long as your word is a recognizable word it won't be corrected, so if you type 'their' instead of 'there' the spellchecker would be happy with that too. More advanced packages will pick up some of these possible mistakes and ask you which word you mean. If you're concerned about spelling, you might consider having speech output software as well.

If you intend to buy a small, portable spellchecker and want to use it in exams, make sure that the one you choose will be permitted. Some of them are quite basic and give only the correct spelling, others give a definition as well.

5.5.2 Meaning

Some hand-held spellcheckers have a built-in dictionary that gives definitions. You can also get good dictionaries on CD-ROM, which you can load into your computer. If you type a word or highlight it in the text you're reading, you can call up the dictionary to get the full definition or, if you have speech output, to check the pronunciation.

5.5.3 Finding the right word

A thesaurus is a dictionary of synonyms – words or phrases that have the same or similar meaning. A thesaurus is very useful for finding a more appropriate word, or finding an alternative when you've used a particular word too often. Using one will help you to increase your vocabulary and improve the quality of your written work. Some word-processor packages include a thesaurus but, like dictionaries, it is possible to get excellent ones on CD-ROM.

5.6 Help with organizing ideas

Software packages designed to help you to organize your ideas are sometimes based on mindmaps; others draw flow diagrams, or allow you to brainstorm, sort and order your ideas. New products are always coming onto the market, so we suggest that you discuss your needs with a specialist such as iANSYST (see section 7.2). Browse in local computer centres. Some packages have free 'tasters' on the internet.

As we prepare this book (October 2000) we think that it's worth looking at:

> *Inspiration* Easy to use and very visual
>
> *Mind Manager* For authentic Buzan 'mindmaps'
>
> *Wordswork* For hints and tips on study skills
>
> *Writer's Toolkit* For help with structuring your work

Standard software packages such as Word and Excel also come with useful drawing and organizing facilities.

5.7 The internet

The internet will give you access to a huge amount of information, advice, dictionaries, encyclopaedias, reference works and websites of every kind. Many websites are ephemeral – here today and gone tomorrow – or are allowed to fall out of date. You may have no way of assessing their quality, but don't be put off. Use the internet intelligently, just as you would a library. If you find a site that you'd like to return to, add it to your *Bookmarks* or *Favourites*. We have listed some of our favourite sites in section 7.3 (page 72).

6.1 Which of your students are dyslexic?

In the first section of this book we saw that dyslexia is likely to affect language, short-term memory, and managing information. Dyslexic students tend to be holistic rather than sequential thinkers. They may be very good at seeing connections but find it difficult to break things down into steps. Some may seem disorganized, and have trouble finding papers or pieces of information. This may cause them to be late with their work or to miss a tutorial.

Difficulties in linguistic coding can interfere with automatic processing when dealing with the written word. Dyslexic students are likely to take longer to put verbal information into their long-term memory or to retrieve it. They may rely more heavily on meaning and understanding. They may also have less effective short-term memories, which affects the ease with which information is held and facts memorized.

You may be puzzled by a student who is articulate and fluent verbally, demonstrating ability to understand concepts and ideas, yet is unable to present the same material on paper. The writing may be disjointed, as if the very ideas have become muddled. The sequencing may be less clear, the vocabulary more restricted. The spelling of individual words may show letter reversals or additions, while some words may be missing all together.

You may notice	Implications
Handwriting May be not joined up, use upper-case letters, look very untidy, with uneven spacing or letters of unequal size.	May be physically taxing, taking so much concentration to form the letters that the thought gets lost.
Spelling May make the work hard to decipher	Vocabulary may be restricted to words more easily spelt.
Written work Incomplete sentences, too many ideas in one sentence, poor selection between less and more important points. Random punctuation, ineffective proofreading.	Slow retrieval of the right words, so the train of thought is lost.
Reading Students may spend hours on allotted reading, complain of difficulties in remembering or comprehending, may misread.	Decoding words distracts from the sense of a passage. Words seem unfamiliar (because of short-term memory difficulties) and have to be repeatedly looked up.
Note-taking Any notes you see may be patchy, with main points not identified. Students say they find it very hard to listen and write simultaneously and sometimes can't read their own notes	Effort of copying from a board or taking notes from a speaker detracts from comprehension.
Oral skills Students may struggle to find the right words, or mispronounce polysyllabic words. They may not follow discussion quickly enough.	Difficulty in pronouncing unfamiliar words may reduce confidence in expressing ideas. Energy expended in auditory processing is taken away from the discussion.
Organization Bringing wrong materials to tutorials, submitting work late, difficulty in following directions.	The more holistic approach isn't suited to categorization of information and of time.

The grammar and spellcheckers that word-processors have can correct a lot of errors and so disguise dyslexic characteristics. Good friends often provide a proofreading service too. This is wonderful and helpful for dyslexics, but it may mean that their difficulties go unnoticed or underestimated.

6.1.1 Assessing dyslexia

Many students will say on their application forms that they have dyslexia: they are strongly encouraged to do so. Others will mention it at some stage during the application or preparation period. But dyslexia is sometimes suggested just by the way they write or say something. Application forms and the first examples of course work can make you aware that a student may be dyslexic. Some characteristic features to look out for are set out in section 1.3, and you can get more ideas from your Regional Centre. Other resources include:

Student handout no. 20 'Dyslexia Checklist' from the Open Teaching Toolkit *Effective Use of English*, Open University.

'Am I dyslexic?' from *Demystifying Dyslexia*, Krupska and Klein.

 t may be quite difficult, and perhaps inappropriate, to suggest dyslexia to a student. If any students ask you whether you think they might be dyslexic, or tell you that they wonder whether they are, you can use the dyslexia checklist from the *Effective Use of English* toolkit to go through the difficulties they mention. You can ask your Regional Centre for a more detailed checklist, or refer the student to a member of Regional Centre staff to talk it through.

Otherwise, you can begin by asking what the student thinks is causing the difficulties and talk about earlier educational experiences. This strategy often elicits a mention of dyslexia. It's important to bear in mind that dyslexia has, in the past, been associated with very negative attitudes and that some people may not be able to cope with the 'label' without some specialized counselling. Your line manager should be able to recommend an appropriate person to help with this.

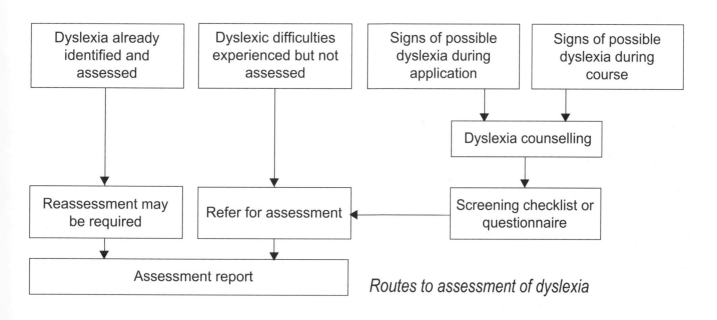

Routes to assessment of dyslexia

6.2 Working with different learners

It's not as necessary to understand dyslexia as to respond to your students' individual learning needs. If a student has a poor short-term memory, takes longer to assimilate new vocabulary, or spends twice the average time reading, you can help enormously by providing appropriate kinds of support. *Some of your other students may share these difficulties to some extent, and others may be dyslexic without recognizing it, so your strategies can benefit everyone.*

Talk to your dyslexic students to help them to be clear about what their areas of difficulty are. You could encourage them to try Activity 1 as a way in. A good starting point is to explore with your students what they find most difficult and what they do best. You may be able to see how you can adapt your teaching style to chime in with their learning styles.

To get the discussion going you could take some ideas from the activities we suggest here, either in an additional session or for 15 minutes at a tutorial, picking it up again at the next.

Activities

1 Ask students to describe how they started their most recent piece of work. Did they decide to record what they did? At what point? Did they write anything down? Did they use a highlighter or underline anything?

2 Make a list of the main activities they undertook. Encourage them to be as specific as possible. Ask them what they found most and least useful.

3 Ask students to write down the thing they enjoyed most in studying, and the thing they liked least.

   Make a list from answers to all these questions, and discuss possible strategies for overcoming problems, or working to students' strengths.

4 Present a page of notes set out both in a linear fashion and in a more diagrammatic style. Choose a section of the course material for this purpose, so that students can see what the original looked like.

   Ask them to choose the layout they prefer, and to try making notes in the same form from another section of the course. Invite them to show you the notes for a brief review of their effectiveness.

5 Ask students to keep a record of what they do each day. You could hand out a week-planner with a space for each day where they can briefly note what they did and how. This can be the basis for a useful support session.

6.3 Strategies for tutors

6.3.1 Additional sessions

Additional sessions are invaluable for many students but may be a lifeline to a dyslexic student. They offer opportunities to

- Go over an area the student needs help in understanding.
- Work together on organization of material.
- Provide an overview of the structure of the course.
- Develop study skills and strategies.
- Help your student to sort out the organizational tasks. For dyslexic students, with their reading and organizational difficulties, the vast amount of general information the Open University sends out in letters, leaflets, booklets and other documents is often the area most neglected.

6.3.2 Organization

Dyslexic students may miss deadlines because their sense of time is less strong, so repetition and reminders of important dates will be helpful. Also remind them how they can get in touch with you if they have a problem. Try:

- Explaining and outlining timetables, dates and instructions.
- Providing one-page information sheets, set out with bullet points, of key dates and related details. A sheet with the tutorials and their topics, together with your telephone number and the best times to contact you, would be useful.

6.3.3 Constructive comment

Follow your usual good practice, only more so. Don't make heavy weather of spelling errors. Ask whether the student would like you to indicate them all or not, and what's the most helpful way of doing so. You might want to discuss this with someone. Some courses may have particular language requirements. There are some useful ideas in the Open University Toolkit *Effective Use of English*.

- Any suggestions for improvement, where a point could be clarified and so on, should be accompanied by as clear a directive as possible. Avoid phrases like 'more detail needed here' without some hint of where the detail might be found.

- Concentrate on one or two areas for improvement at a time.

- Write your comments clearly.

- Give examples to make your meaning plain.

6.3.4 At tutorials, day-schools and residential schools

- Outline the running order at the beginning of the tutorial. This kind of framework helps holistic thinkers. Break the session up so there are gaps for students to finish off notes or ask questions.

- Present your material in a variety of ways: diagrams, colourful handouts, tapes, three-dimensional and tactile.

- It helps more holistic thinkers if you move from the whole to the parts, then make connections between them, adding concrete examples to flesh out abstract ideas.

- Use the board to highlight important concepts, definitions and new terms, so that students can make more effective notes. Write in large clear letters.

- Use small groups to offer the opportunity for students to go over and clarify what is being discussed.

- Try not to ask students to respond to new pieces of reading on the spot, nor to work on handouts immediately in a group. Build in some reading time if you can.

- Offer students different ways of taking part, so that nervous students aren't forced to read out something out they've just written or to make an immediate response to a discussion.

- Keep overhead projections brief, and provide photocopies.

6.3.5 Handouts

Give out brief handouts outlining key points:

- Try alternative layouts. Some students may welcome a mindmap or more visual outline of the points.

- Put any notes you are providing on coloured paper. Some dyslexic students find pale blue or yellow much easier to read.

- Use a plain typeface (Arial is often preferred) and a slightly larger print size (enlarge photocopies if possible). Keep lines of print reasonably short (easier to track), and space out your notes as much as you can. Ask students about their preferences.

6.3.6 Written work

- Offer some short examples of written work.
- Refer students to the Student Toolkits or to study skill materials on essay-writing.
- Offer models of reports, projects etc., and examples of plans or outlines.

When it comes to writing assignments:

- Make sure that all instructions and advice in the assignment guide are fully understood.
- Clarify terms such as 'discuss', 'compare' and so on.
- Suggest ways of making a plan.

6.3.7 Revision and examinations

The time limit in an examination is particularly difficult for anyone who reads more slowly, so encourage students to ask for extra time if they need it.

- Dyslexic students are more likely to misread a question, so practise looking at questions with them.
- Encourage them to practise planning and writing short answers during their revision, keeping to a time limit. Under pressure their writing can really deteriorate. Offer your comments on their work.

Above all, encourage. It's hard being an OU student at the best of times, and harder still if certain tasks take twice as long.

Help your students to use their study time as effectively as possible.

Spending time on strategy will pay off.

SECTION 7
RESOURCES

7.1. BOOKS

7.1.1 For students

Every Letter Counts – Winning in Life Despite Dyslexia, Susan Hampshire, 1984, Bantam Press. Several useful descriptions of dyslexic adults, and some advice about strategy.

The Dyslexia Handbook, published regularly by the British Dyslexia Association. Short sections on a wide variety of topics from spelling and computing to examinations and the Education Act.

7.1.2 For tutors

Adult Dyslexia: Assessment, Counselling and Training, McLoughlin, Fitzgibbon and Young, 1994, Whurr. A useful book for tutors and counsellors. Suggests assessment and diagnostic strategies.

Diagnosing Dyslexia, Cynthia Klein, 1993, ALBSU. A short book designed to offer tutors in adult, further and higher education materials for diagnosing students. Has a useful chapter on talking to students about dyslexia.

Specific Learning Difficulties (Dyslexia), P. Pumfrey and R. Reason, 1991, Routledge. Covers every possible aspect of dyslexia – educational, psychological and medical. Also looks at schools, exam boards and government.

Drawing on the Right Side of the Brain, Betty Edwards, 1981, Souvenir Press. Explains the wide range of abilities of the brain, and offers interesting strategies to help with verbal tasks.

Writing and the Writer, Frank Smith, 1982, Heinemann. A fascinating and thoughtful examination of everything that writing involves for the writer, such as the difference between composition and transcription, the thought processes behind language and the differences between spoken and written language.

How to Detect and Manage Dyslexia, Philomena Ott, 1997, Heinemann. Useful for general reference.

7.1.3 Spelling

Look at a few spelling dictionaries before you decide which to buy. People's preferences do differ. If you're likely to use one in an exam, make sure you choose one that will be allowed.

The Ace Spelling Dictionary, David Moseley and Catherine Nical, LDA, Duke Street, Wisbech, Cambridgeshire.

Spelling List for Dyslexics, obtainable from Mrs E. Stirling, St David's College, Llandudno, Gwynedd.

The Pergamon Dictionary of Perfect Spelling, ed. Christine Maxwell. Available at good bookshops.

Hamlyn's Good Spelling Dictionary, Hamlyn, 1979. Good – gives all parts of a word, e.g. give, giving, gave.

Signposts to Spelling, Joy Pollock, 1980. An inexpensive spelling guide first published by the Helen Arkell Centre for Dyslexia. Especially useful for teachers.

Spelling Checklist, E. Stirling, 1984, St David's College, Llandudno, Gwynedd. A mini-dictionary of 726 words (common irregulars, similar words etc.).

Which is Witch, E. Stirling, 1984, St David's College, Llandudno, Gwynedd. A very useful little booklet of common homonyms, with meanings and a brief phrase showing usage.

Unscrambling Spelling, C. Klein and R. Miller, 1990, Hodder and Stoughton.

7.1.4 Study skills

It would be impossible to review even a substantial proportion of all the books available. Here is a selection:

The Good Study Guides, The Open University. Very well structured guides to writing, reading, organizing notes etc. Can be used for reference or as workbooks:

The Good Study Guide, Andrew Northedge, 1990, The Open University

The Arts Good Study Guide, Andrew Northedge and Ellie Chambers, The Open University

The Science Good Study Guide, Andrew Northedge, Jeff Thomas, Andrew Lane and Alice Peasgood, The Open University

Rediscover Grammar, David Crystal, 1994, Longmans. A really entertaining book that starts from scratch.

The Study Skills Handbook, Stella Cottrell, 1999, Macmillan. An excellent book for all students in higher education. Well presented and includes lots of ideas for tackling a range of difficulties and improving study skills. Stella is a university lecturer and is dyslexic herself.

Use Your Head, T. Buzan, 1986, BBC Books.

Use Your Memory, T. Buzan, 1986, BBC Books.

The Mindmap Book, T. Buzan, 1993, BBC Books. Perhaps best known for his mindmaps, Buzan offers some really interesting ways of learning and structuring memory. Many students find his ideas particularly useful.

Your Memory. A User's Guide, A. Baddeley, 1994, Penguin. This fascinating book (update of the original in 1982) explains how your memory works, as well as offering strategies to improve learning and memory.

Introducing Neuro-Linguistic Programming, Joseph O'Connor and John Seymour, 1990, Crucible. An excellent introduction to the field of neurolinguistic programming (NLP). Also lists NLP organizations and gives a guide to NLP publications for specific applications.

7.2 Organizations offering advice for dyslexic students

Adult Dyslexia Organisation

336 Brixton Road   *Helpline* 020 7924 9559
London   *Admin* 020 7737 7646
SW9 7AA   *Fax* 020 7207 7796
E-mail dyslexia.hq@dial.pipex.com

A helpful, professional and friendly organization for adults who have dyslexia, professionals and others with an interest in adults. Publishes regular newsletters, factsheets, guidance notes and so on, and runs meetings and conferences. A registered charity.

British Dyslexia Association

98 London Road   *Helpline* 01189 668 271
Reading   *Fax* 01189 351 927
Berks
RG1 5AU
E-mail bda_dyslexia@cix.compulink.co.uk

Concentrates mainly on children but also has some useful
factsheets for adults. Many local branches, some of which
have adult groups. Useful for assessments and learning skills
support. A lot of information is available from the website – see
section 7.3.

Skill (National Bureau for Disabled Students)

Chapter House   *Tel.* 020 7450 0620
18–20 Crucifix Lane   *Fax* 020 7450 0650
London SE1 3JW

Dyslexia Institute

133 Gresham Road   *Tel.* 01784 463 851
Staines   *Fax* 01784 460 747
Middlesex
TW18 2AJ

Offers training for teachers of dyslexics, assessments and
tuition. Has 26 centres nationwide.

Adult Dyslexia and Skills Development Centre

5 Tavistock Place   *Tel.* 020 7388 8744
London
WC1H 9SN

Offers assessment and tuition.

iANSYST

The White House   *Tel.* 01223 42 01 01
72 Fen Road   *Freephone* 0500 14 15 15
Cambridge
CB4 1UN
E-mail sales@dyslexic.com

National and international experts in equipment and software
for dyslexics. Very helpful organization that can help you to
decide on the best computer packages for you.

7.3 Websites

Here are some websites that we have found interesting and useful. Some are very well designed and allow you to change the font and colour to suit yourself. Two warnings, though:

■ Websites change and fall out of date, so use your search engine to look out for new ones. We recommend *www.google.com/*, a very fast and comprehensive search engine. Just type in that address and follow the instructions.

■ It's very easy to make a mistake when typing in web addresses. We strongly suggest that when you find a useful site you 'bookmark' the address, so that you never have to type it in again!

www.bda-dyslexia.org.uk/
  The British Dyslexia Association's website. Lots of useful information for and about dyslexics.

www.disinhe.ac.uk
  The higher education community's centre for disability information.

www.futurenet.co.uk/charity/ado/adomenu/adomenu.htm The Adult Dyslexia Organisation website. Still young, but developing.

www.surrey.ac.uk/Psychology/WDNF/front.html Developed by Ian Smythe and Andrew Barnes of Surrey University. Offers advice sheets, conferences and other information about dyslexia, and has many links to other sites. Includes information about the World Dyslexia Network Foundation (WDNF) Some pages are outdated, but the WDNF pages are well designed.

freespace.virgin.net/peter.hill7/dyshelp/index.htm
  Peter Hill's website. Includes downloadable help sheets to aid those who are dyslexic or who have sensory or motor control difficulties in getting the most out of Windows 95 and Microsoft Word.

www.dyslexia-advice.com/
  Philomena Ott's website. Limited, but has a newsletter and a page about her book.

www.pottage.demon.co.uk/it-helps/index.html
  Ted Pottage's home page, with links to other sites. Ted is dyslexic and an enthusiast about the positive aspects of dyslexia.

Technological information

www.dyslexic.com
> Information about computers and software for dyslexics. This is the iANSYST home page. Has useful links to other sites.

www.abilitynet.co.uk
> Helpful information and tips about technology.

www.dyslexia.com/
> A US website based on Ron Davis's ideas and his book *The Gift of Dyslexia.* There is a discussion board for all to join in, and access to information and articles. Well designed and easy to navigate.

7.4 Open University resources

A wide range of services, facilities and support is available to Open University students. They are described in the suite of booklets:

Meeting Your Needs

Meeting Your Residential School Needs

Meeting Your Exam Needs

If you are an OU student, make sure that you have all these.

7.5 Disabled Students' Allowances (DSAs)

Open University students in England, Wales and Northern Ireland (and in Scotland from 2002, possibly) are eligible for DSAs. They can be used to pay for equipment and facilities related to your dyslexia, but not for the cost of identifying (diagnosing) it. Details will be sent to students who have told the University that they are dyslexic, but you will need a diagnostic assessment if you want to claim DSAs.

Proofreading checklist

THE WORDS

1 Proofread for grammatical errors

a Has every sentence got a subject and a verb?

b Are the verbs the right tense (present, past, future)?

c Are adjectives and adverbs used correctly?

d Are there too many clauses or ideas in one sentence – is the sentence too long?

2 Proofread for spelling mistakes

a Look carefully at each word. It sometimes helps to start at the end of your text and read backwards – you then see each word on its own.

b Underline any word that looks wrong.

c Check the spelling in the dictionary.

d Beware – word-processor spellcheckers only recognize misspellings. They don't know if 'off' has been used instead of 'of', or 'hear' instead of 'here'.

3 Proofread for punctuation mistakes

a Full stop at end of sentence, capital letter at beginning?

b Clauses or phrases will probably need commas to separate them from the main sentence.

c Are apostrophes correct?

d Are any ?s or !s needed?

> *Don't think about these points while you're writing.*
> *That will slow down your flow of ideas.*
> *Proofread when you've finished.*

THE CONTENT

4 Proofreading for content

It helps to read your work out loud. You can read it on to tape and then play it back, or get someone else to do that for you. Listening to your writing helps you to spot things that might not make sense. Have a draft copy of your essay in one hand and a pencil in the other to note mistakes.

General points

a Is each sentence clear?

b Have you missed out any essential information?

c Will your reader know what you mean?

d Are you using a particular word too often? Can you think of another one to use?

Introduction

e Has your work got a beginning? It should be a short paragraph that tells the reader what you're going to say and roughly how you're going to say it.

f Are you going to make any assumptions? State them clearly in your introduction.

The main part of the essay

g Have you given an explanation for every assertion you've made?

Conclusions

h Has your work got an ending? Your last paragraph should draw together everything you've said. It should also answer the question. A reader who looks only at the title and the conclusions should be in no doubt what your views are, though without knowing why you came to those conclusions.

Activity 3
Your preferred learning style

There are many kinds of learning style. Some people prefer to do most of their learning on their own, others thrive by bouncing ideas off each other in groups. Some people work much better at home, others prefer to find a working environment like a reference library where everyone else is working too. Some like to ask for support when they need it, others like directed encouragement. We all lean towards different styles according to the task in hand. When it comes to using our senses we tend to have a preferred way of learning.

We learn by using our senses – seeing, hearing and doing (smelling and touching can be grouped with 'doing'). Many people use these senses equally and often together. These people are 'multi-sensory learners'. Some people employ one or two senses more than the others. Understanding how you do things can guide you to your preferred way of learning.

Try the questions in Sections A, B and C of this activity. Put a tick in one of the columns for each question. Then see what *Interpreting your results* tells you about your preferred learning style.

SECTION A

Do you ...	1 Yes – often	2 Seldom or never
Understand complex or academic topics better by listening to someone rather than by reading?		
Learn to spell new words by saying the letters or syllables out loud rather than by writing them down?		
Prefer to listen to a talk rather than read about the topic?		
Need to have graphs or diagrams explained verbally?		
Tend to hum or talk to yourself?		
Take in details about news items better by listening to the radio rather than from a newspaper?		
Tend to use expressions like 'I hear what you're saying', 'That sounds good', 'I like the sound of that' etc.?		
Prefer to have background music on while reading?		
Can you ...		
Remember sounds you've heard in the past, when you hear them again?		
Remember more about a topic by listening rather than by reading about it?		
Understand and remember oral directions or instructions better than written ones?		
Total		

SECTION B

Do you ...	1 Yes – often	2 Seldom or never
Prefer to write down things that you need to remember or learn?		
Remember something by imagining a picture or diagram in your head?		
Enjoy drawing maps, graphs and charts?		
Prefer to have directions or instructions written down with diagrams rather than deal with oral directions?		
Remember something by seeing it like a picture in your head?		
Give examples that are very pictorial when describing something or someone?		
Tend to remember faces but forget names?		
Regularly use phrases like 'imagine it', 'see that' etc.?		
Can you ...		
Understand maps and follow directions from a map or diagram?		
Follow a news item better on TV than radio?		
Remember where you saw something on a page in a book, or visualize the exact location of a remembered object?		
Total		

SECTION C

Do you ...	1 Yes – often	2 Seldom or never
Tend to press hard when writing so that there's an impression of what you've written on the next page?		
Like making things and working with tools of various kinds?		
Tend to walk about while thinking, or find it difficult to sit still for very long?		
Tend to fiddle with things when you're thinking or speaking?		
Nibble, smoke or fidget with objects when you're reading or studying?		
Like doing jigsaw puzzles, Chinese puzzles or mazes?		
Feel OK touching others, hugging etc.?		
Use expressions such as 'I need to get the feel of that', 'I need to get a grip on that'?		
Want to touch objects rather than just look at them?		
Can you ...		
Remember things better if you write them down over and over again?		
Learn the spelling of new words better by tracing out the shape of the letters with your fingers?		
Total		

INTERPRETING YOUR RESULTS

Add up the number of ticks in column one and enter the totals in the table below:

	Section A	Section B	Section C
Number of ticks in column 1			

- If you have more* ticks in Section A than in B or C, you probably learn best by hearing – you are an audio learner.

- If you have more* ticks in Section B than in A or C, you probably learn best by seeing – you are a visual learner.

- If you have more ticks in Section C than in B or A, you probably learn best by doing – you are a 'kinaesthetic' or 'tactile' learner.

- If you have roughly* the same number of ticks in Sections A and B, you probably learn equally by seeing and hearing – you are an audio-visual learner.

- If you have roughly* the same number of ticks in Sections A and C, you probably learn equally by doing and hearing – you are an audio-kinaesthetic learner.

- If you have roughly* the same number of ticks in Sections B and C, you probably learn equally by doing and seeing – you are a visual-kinaesthetic learner.

- If you have roughly* the same number of ticks in all three sections, you are probably a multi-sensory learner and learn equally well by hearing, seeing and doing.

[* 'Roughly' means totals within 3 ticks of each other. 'More' means at least 3 ticks more.]

Think about the questions and your answers after you've completed the activity. They'll help you to develop your own strategies for learning. We have suggested some ideas for learning strategies at the end of this activity, and you'll be able to think of more. Note the things that work really well for you and devise ways of using these strengths to approach your learning tasks.

STRATEGIES FOR HELPING LEARNING AND WRITING TASKS

Here are some ideas for the planning and initial stage of working on an assignment. They have been developed with dyslexic students. You can adapt these or add your own.

For visual learners – working through seeing

Try using mindmaps. They don't have to be like Tony Buzan's: try designing your own.

Use colour coding to link similar ideas.

Finding it hard to put things into words? Make a diagram or adapt one from your book. You can then refer to it in your text.

Use 'post-its' for notes, for brainstorming, for marking pages. They come in different colours.

Make posters about the subject. You can use drawing or pictures as well as words.

For auditory learners – working through hearing

Put your ideas on to audio-tape.

Talk your ideas out loud to yourself as if discussing with someone, and record what you say.

Discuss your ideas with someone.

Use a computer with voice recognition.

Plan an essay as if you were giving a talk.

Work with music in the background.

Work from recorded books.

For kinaesthetic (tactile) learners – working through doing

Interact with the materials you're using.

Put your ideas on to index cards.

Use a computer programme such as *Thinksheet* or *Inspiration* to plan your work.

Cut up photocopies of relevant parts of texts or newspaper articles.

Try making a collage mindmap, using pictures associated with ideas.

Walk about while you're thinking.

Take regular breaks and do something physical in them.

Try ideas out, or imagine yourself or someone else doing something.

For multisensory learners

Choose what you feel best with.

For all learners
Break tasks down into small chunks

Activity 4
Right brain – left brain

1 When planning an essay, report or talk do you usually

a   Make a list?

b   Start with a diagram or mindmap?

c   No strong preference?

2 When you're describing something to someone do you prefer to

a   Use words to define what you mean?

b   Use a diagram or drawing, or supplement your words with your hands?

c   No strong preference?

3 When going into a strange room do you tend to

a   Notice particular things or details?

b   Get a feeling of the effect of the whole room?

c   No strong preference?

4 If you're faced with a complicated task do you

a   Start by quickly breaking it down into smaller tasks and putting those in order?

b   Find it difficult to know where to begin but still have an appreciation that it can be done?

c   No strong preference?

5 Faced with a difficult situation that needs to be put right would you

a   Try to sort out the cause and effects?

b   Be looking at the interrelationships between all the parts?

c   No strong preference?

6 Would you describe yourself as someone who makes decisions by

a   A stepwise process of deduction?

b   Intuitively?

c   No strong preference?

7 When you recount a story to friends do you tend to

a   Keep to the facts?

b   Make a lot of elaborations?

c   No strong preference?

8 What are you best at doing

a   Remembering sequences?

b   Remembering images?

c   No strong preference?

9 Would you describe yourself as

a   Better at making ideas work?

b   Better at coming up with ideas?

c   No strong preference?

10 Do you know where everything is on your desk or other personal space

a   Because it's reasonably tidy and well-ordered?

b   In spite of its being untidy?

c   No strong preference?

11 Do you remember things best if they are

a   In some order such as by date, alphabetical etc.?

b   In the form of a diagram or picture?

c   No strong preference?

12 Do you prefer to use

a   Flow diagrams?

b   Mindmaps?

c   No strong preference?

13 What do you remember most easily in songs

a   The words?

b   The rhythm and music?

c   No strong preference?

14 What do you remember best

a   Names?

b   Faces?

c   No strong preference?

YOUR ANSWERS

Mostly a or many more a than b
You are clearly more left-brained and you could learn best through words, lists, ordering things logically.

Mostly b or more b than a
You are clearly more right-brained and you could learn best through colour, shape, patterns and tunes.

Mostly c or roughly equal a and b
You show no particular preference and could use a wide range of strategies for learning.